New Creations
ADULT COLORING
BOOK SERIES

To see original photographs
please go to:

www.facebook.com/groups/newcreationscoloring

"...the old is gone, all things are are made new."

2 Cor. 5:17

New Creations
ADULT COLORING
BOOK SERIES

This Book
Belongs To:

_____

"...the old is gone, all things
are are made new."

2 Cor. 5:17

_____
Date

Other coloring books are available from

New Creations Coloring Book Series:

Animals Architecture Birds 2018 Calender Christmas Christmas Cards Churches

Dinosaurs Easter Fall Fashion Flowers Holiday Insects Kids A Coloring Mix Nature

People Santa Scenic Scripture Seasons Snowmen Transportation Tropical Vintage

Water Winter

Be sure to collect them all.

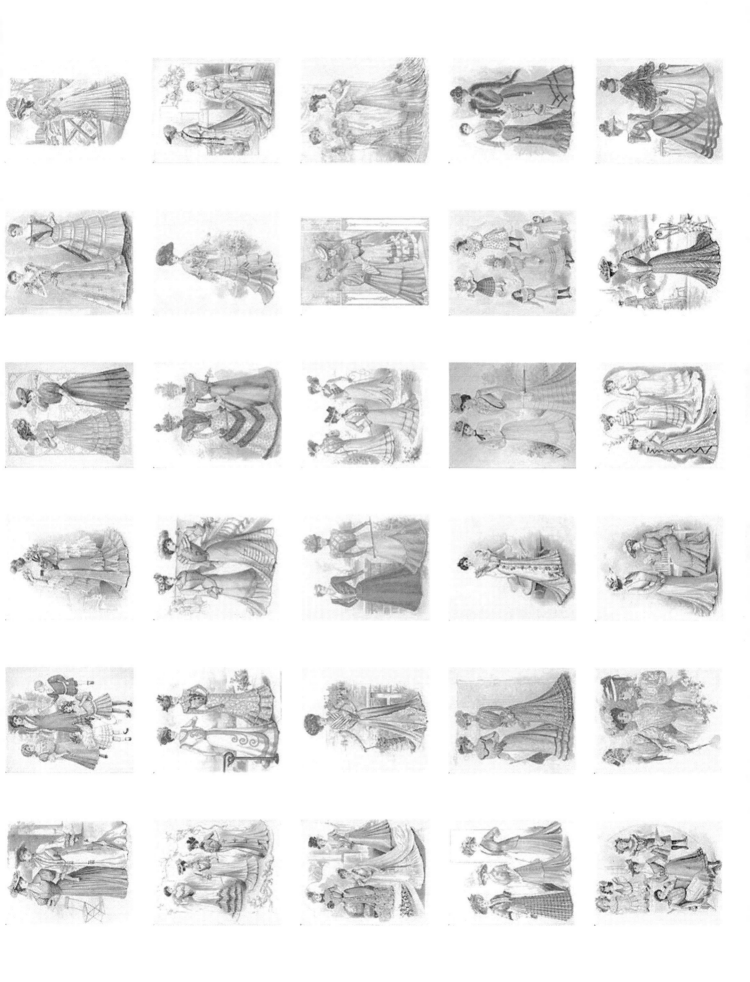

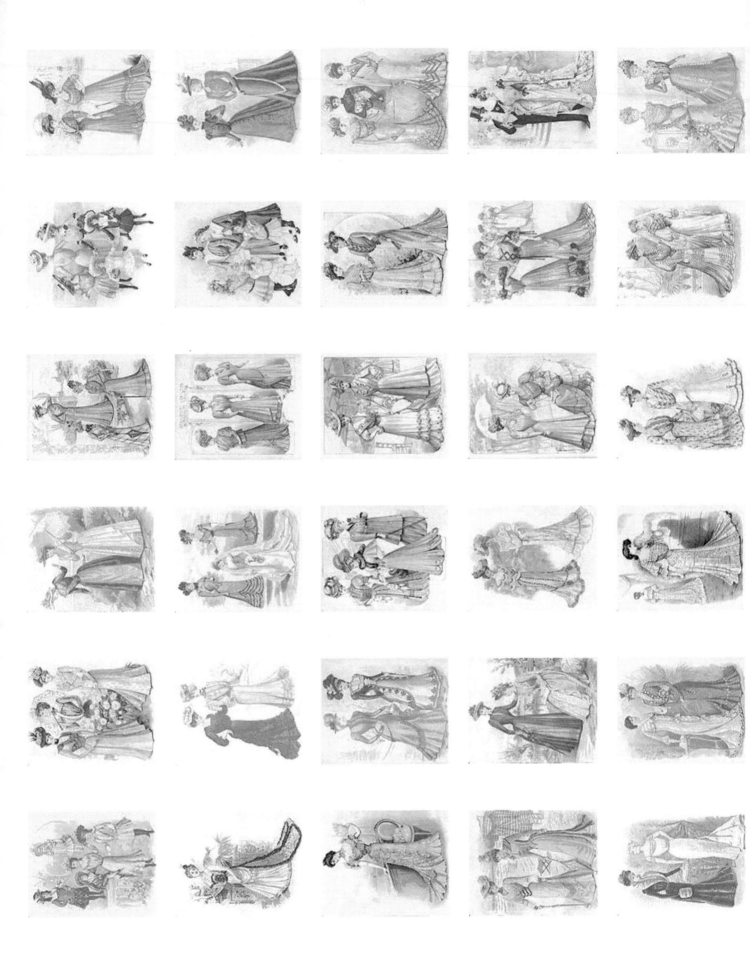

Dr. Teresa Davis has her doctorate degree in counseling and is the Executive Director of a non-profit Christian counseling center. As a counselor, she learned how coloring helps reduce stress, increase focus, minimize pain, and encourages imagination. As a lifetime amateur photographer she has a library of photos including over 100,000 pictures she has taken since receiving her first DSLR camera as a gift in 2007. In 2016, Teresa was intrigued when saw her first grayscale coloring page, realizing she had a pot of grayscale gold contained within several external hard drives. New Creations Adult Coloring Book Series is the result of many hours searching through those hard drives to find just the right shots from photos she has taken during her worldwide travels.

Teresa has been married to her husband Brad for 40 years. They have 2 married sons and 4 teenage grandsons. She is also crafter of all sorts, seamstress, quilter, and recycler. In addition, she is a licensed and ordained minister, a public speaker, conference and retreat leader, and teacher.

207X.   208X.

Made in the USA
San Bernardino, CA
22 May 2018